The Old-Time Television Trivia Book II

ALSO BY MEL SIMONS:

The Old-Time Radio Trivia Book

The Old-Time Television Trivia Book

Old-Time Radio Memories

The Show-Biz Trivia Book

Old-Time Television Memories

The Movie Trivia Book

Voices From the Philco

The Good Music Trivia Book

The Mel Simons Joke Book

The Old-Time Radio Trivia Book II

The Comedians Trivia Book

The Old-Time Radio Trivia Book III

Take These Jokes Please

The Old-Time Radio Trivia Book IV

The Old-Time Television Trivia Book II

by Mel Simons

BearManor Media
2016

The Old-Time Television Trivia Book II

© 2016 Mel Simons

For information, address:

BearManor Media
P. O. Box 71426
Albany, GA 31708

bearmanormedia.com

Typesetting and layout by John Teehan

Published in the USA by BearManor Media

ISBN — 978-1-62933-081-5

Dedication

This book is dedicated to Morgan White, Jr. Morgan who is a master of trivia.

I have been a regular on his radio show on WBZ for many years. I consider Morgan one of my closest friends.

Mel Simons
www.melsimons.net

Frank Avruch

Foreword

MEL SIMONS IS THE "KING OF TRIVIA."

Just ask anyone who has been to one of his shows, or who has read his books on the subject. It is his passion, and he has spent almost all his adult life perfecting his craft. His latest trivia book concentrates on some of the most famous celebrities from the old television days, people like Milton Berle, Sid Caesar, Imogene Coca, and let's not forget the Lone Ranger and Tonto. An avid collector, Mel has included some of his prized celebrity autographed pictures and other memorabilia. He definitely was a saver.

He has met many of the TV stars he writes about; many have become good friends. As you venture through the golden age of television and many different trivia quizzes, you're in for a learning and fun experience. As someone who has spent time presenting movies from Hollywood's Golden Age, I picked up a lot of old movie trivia. Now I can include TV trivia as well.

One last trivia question to Mr. Simons, if I may: Who was the nationally-syndicated Bozo the Clown?

Frank Avruch
WCVB's "Goodwill Ambassador"
and "Man About Town"

1

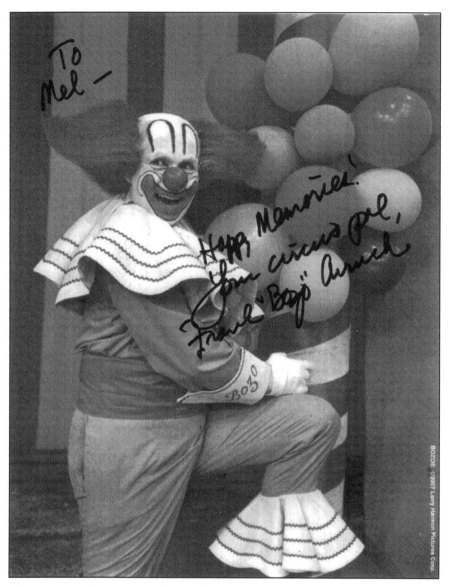

Frank Avrush as Bozo the Clown

Kukla, Fran and Ollie

Jon Provost and Lassie

Quiz #1

MULTIPLE CHOICE
(Answers on page 125)

1. Who played Mr. Wizard?
   a) Don Herbert   b) Monty Hall   c) Hal Smith

2. Paul Harvey was based in what city?
   a) Philadelphia   b) Chicago   c) Los Angeles

3. Who played Dr. Richard Kimble on The Fugitive?
   a) Ben Casey   b) David Janssen   c) Van Heflin

4. Bruce Lee starred in which TV show?
   a) *Charlie Chan*   b) *Kung Fu*   c) *The Green Hornet*

5. Name Sanford's son on Sanford and Son.
   a) Lamont   b) Lester   c) Larry

6. What was the name of the Six Million Dollar Man?
   a) Gregg Austin   b) Steve Myers   c) Steve Austin

7. Jack Lord was the star of which cop show?
   a) *Cannon*   b) *Hawaii Five-O*   c) *Bulldog Drummond*

8. Who played the man on Chico and the Man?
   a) Jack Hynes   b) Jack Albertson   c) Jack Dempsey

9. Name the Marx brother who appeared on I Love Lucy.
   a) Groucho   b) Chico   c) Harpo

10. Harry Morgan did not appear in which show?
    a) *Fish*   b) *M*A*S*H*   c) *December Bride*

Penny arcade cards

Quiz #2

TELEVISION QUOTES
(Answers on page 125)

Match the comedienne with her TV show.

1. "Say, kids, what time is it?"
2. "Just the facts, ma'am."
3. "This tape will self-destruct in 5 seconds."
4. "I swear I'll kill you."
5. "One of these days, Alice, pow! Right in the kisser!"
6. "Ever notice . . ."
7. "Lookin' good."
8. "Would you believe . . ."
9. "Yoohoo, Mrs. Bloom."
10. "Well, gahhhhhh-lee."

a. *The Honeymooners*
b. *Mission: Impossible*
c. *Howdy Doody*
d. *Gomer Pyle, U.S.M.C.*
e. *Get Smart*
f. *Sixty Minutes*
g. *Dragnet*
h. *Chico and the Man*
i. *The Goldbergs*
j. *Texaco Star Theatre*

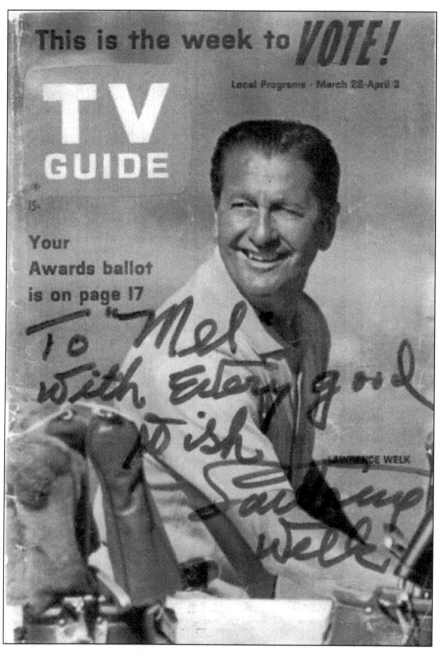

Lawrence Welk

Quiz #3

LAWRENCE WELK
(Answers on Page 126)

1. Lawrence played which musical instrument?
2. He was known for playing what type of music?
3. The television show came from what ballroom?
4. Name the singing sisters who were regulars on the how.
5. What were their first names?
6. What did Lawrence say to start every song?
7. Name his first champagne lady.
8. Who was his long-time sponsor?
9. Name his musical director.
10. Who was the dancer who was once a Mouseketeer?

Red Skelton

Quiz #4

RED SKELTON
(Answers on Page 126)

1. What is Red's real first name?
2. How many years was he on television?
3. What was his theme song?
4. Name his long-time orchestra leader.
5. What was the name of the punch-drunk boxer that Red always did?
6. Name the drunk character that he did.
7. What was that character's most famous routine?
8. Name the two sea gulls.
9. Red was known for painting pictures of what?
10. What did Red always say at the end of his show?

Ralph Edwards

Quiz #5

DETECTIVES
(Answers on Page 126)

Match the detective with the actor.

1. Barnaby Jones
2. Kojak
3. The Thin Man
4. Richard Diamond
5. Baretta
6. Boston Blackie
7. Steve McGarrett
8. Rockford
9. Martin Kane
10. McMillan

a. James Garner
b. Rock Hudson
c. Robert Blake
d. Buddy Ebsen
e. Peter Lawford
f. Jack Lord
g. William Gargan
h. Telly Savalas
i. David Jannsen
j. Kent Taylor

The cast of I've Got a Secret *(left to right: l-to-r: Bill Cullen, Jayne Meadows, Gary Moore, Henry Morgan, Betsy Palmer)*

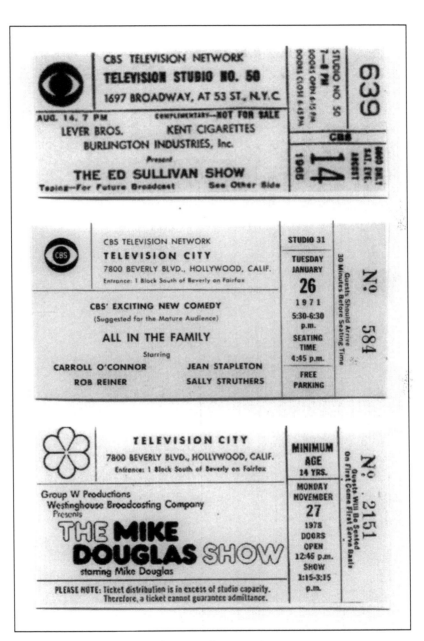

Tickets to television shows

Loretta Young

Quiz #6

WOMEN OF LAUGHTER
(Answers on Page 127)

Match the comedienne with her TV show.

1. Valerie Harper
2. Loretta Swit
3. Gilda Radner
4. Carol Burnett
5. Jean Stapleton
6. Florence Henderson
7. Adrienne Barbeau
8. Nanette Fabray
9. Candice Bergen
10. Julia Louis-Dreyfus

a. *The Brady Bunch*
b. *All in the Family*
c. *M*A*S*H*
d. *Murphy Brown*
e. *Maude*
f. *Rhoda*
g. *The Garry Moore Show*
h. *Saturday Night Live*
i. *Seinfeld*
j. *Caesar's Hour*

Fred MacMurray

Quiz #7

WESTERNS
(Answers on Page 127)

Match the Western with the actor.

1. *Gunsmoke*
2. *Wagon Train*
3. *The Rifleman*
4. *Maverick*
5. *Wild, Wild West*
6. *Sugarfoot*
7. *Tales of Wells Fargo*
8. *Rawhide*
9. *The Life and Legend of Wyatt Earp*
10. *The Virginian*

a. Clint Eastwood
b. James Arness
c. Hugh O'Brian
d. Dale Robertson
e. Robert Conrad
f. Ward Bond
g. James Drury
h. Chuck Connors
i. Will Hutchins
j. James Garner

Mel Simons and Tony Orlando

Quiz #8

GENERAL QUESTIONS
(Answers on Page 127)

1. What was the name of the Sea-Sick Sea Serpent?
2. Who portrayed the grandfather on *My Three Sons*?
3. The "Heart Fund" was a feature on which game show?
4. Molly Goldberg had two children. Name them.
5. What was Kate Smith's theme song?
6. Name the luxurious cruise ship.
7. Mr. Whipple served as a long-time spokesman for which product?
8. Michael Anthony was a character on which show?
9. What is the logo for NBC?
10. Name the show that featured Cubby, Lonnie, and Annette.

Quiz #9

IDENTIFY THE NIGHT OF THE WEEK EACH SHOW WAS ON

(Answers on Page 128)

1. *The Fugitive*
2. *The Red Skelton Show*
3. *What's My Line?*
4. *The Cosby Show*
5. *The Golden Girls*
6. *I've Got a Secret*
7. *The Jack Benny Show*
8. *Batman*
9. *The Perry Como Show*
10. *George Burns and Gracie Allen Show*

Quiz #10

GENERAL QUESTIONS
(Answers on Page 128)

1. Who created Kukla, Fran and Ollie?

2. Name the chimpanzee that was a regular on *The Today Show*.

3. Broderick Crawford starred in which cop show?

4. "The Mouse" was a hit record for which TV comedian?

5. Name the TV personality who was known for showing home movies of celebrities.

6. What did Hal Kanter do for a living?

7. Joan Davis and Jim Backus co-starred on which show?

8. Name the detective show that took place on a house-boat.

9. Who created *The Twilight Zone*?

10. What was Ernie Kovacs' favorite form of tobacco?

Danny Thomas

Quiz #11

DANNY THOMAS
(Answers on Page 128)

1. Where did Danny grow up?

2. What is Danny's real name?

3. Name the movie he starred in that was a remake of an Al Jolson movie.

4. What was the original name of his TV show?

5. Name the members of his first TV family.

6. Name the members of his second TV family.

7. Hans Conreid played what character on the show?

8. Name the nightclub where Danny entertained.

9. Who owned the nightclub?

10. Danny founded what hospital?

Marjorie Lord

Angela Cartwright and Danny Thomas

Rusty Hammer and Danny Thomas

Quiz #12

TRUE OR FALSE
(Answers on Page 129)

1. The sponsor of *I Remember Mama* was Sanka.

2. Edie Adams was married to Ernie Kovacs.

3. FDR was the first president to appear on TV.

4. Dick Cavett was born in Idaho.

5. The co-stars of *Halls of Ivy* were Ronald Coleman and Benita Hume.

6. Sylvester Weaver was the president of CBS.

7. Josephine the Plumber was played by Jane Withers.

8. John Wayne introduced the first episode of *Gunsmoke*.

9. "Oh, My Papa" was a hit record for Perry Como.

10. Barbara Walters was the first female national news anchor.

THE HOLLYWOOD PALACE THEATRE
1735 NORTH VINE STREET
HOLLYWOOD 28, CALIFORNIA

THURSDAY
NOVEMBER
30
1967

ABC TELEVISION NETWORK presents

THE HOLLYWOOD PALACE

JIMMY   DURANTE
Master of Ceremonies
and GUEST STARS

Show Time
6:00 P.M.

Doors Close
5:30 P.M.

Children Under
12 Will Not Be
Admitted

As the audience may be seen on camera we request that the ladies wear dresses, rather than informal attire, and gentlemen wear coats and ties.

CBS TELEVISION NETWORK
TELEVISION CITY
7800 BEVERLY BLVD. HOLLYWOOD, CALIF.
Entrance: 1 Block South of Beverly on Fairfax

STUDIO 33

MONDAY
SEPTEMBER
29
1969
6:30-8:00
p.m.

SEATING
TIME
5:45 p.m.

FREE
PARKING

Guests Should Arrive 30 Minutes Before Seating Time

N°. 448

THE
RED SKELTON
SHOW

Preview Performance

WFIL-TV   46th & Market Streets
Philadelphia 39, Pa.

AMERICAN BANDSTAND
with Dick Clark

American Bandstand is holding a reservation for
you to visit the program on WED JAN 2 1962

Dick Clark

N°. 19221

NOT TRANSFERABLE · VOID IF SOLD · SEE REVERSE SIDE

Tickets to television shows

Quiz #13

DETECTIVES
(Answers on Page 129)

Match the detective with the actor.

1. William Conrad
2. Hal Linden
3. Karl Malden
4. Dennis Franz
5. Ralph Bellamy
6. David Jannsen
7. Roger Moore
8. Burt Reynolds
9. Christopher Meloni
10. Robert Wagner

a. Harry-O
b. Barney Miller
c. Elliott Stabler
d. Andy Sipowitz
e. Mike Stone
f. Cannon
g. Simon Templer
h. Jonathan Hart
i. Mike Barnett
j. Dan August

Phil Silvers

Quiz #14

PHIL SILVERS
(Answers on Page 129)

1.   What was the original name of *The Phil Silvers Show*?

2.   Who created the show?

3.   Name the character that Phil played.

4.   What was his rank?

5.   Name the fort.

6.   Where was the fort located?

7.   Maurice Gosfield played what character?

8.   What was Phil's favorite thing to do?

9.   Paul Ford played what character?

10. Phil had a crush on what WAC?

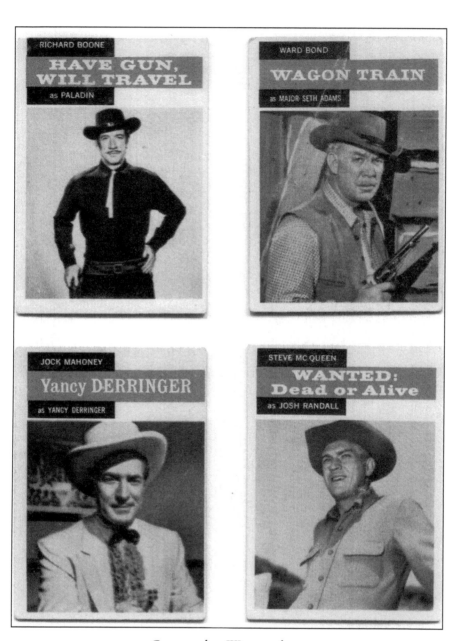

Gum cards – Western shows

Quiz #15

PARTNERS

(Answers on Page 130)

Match the partners.

1. Lucy
2. Clark
3. Siskel
4. Dean
5. Dick
6. Bert
7. Cagney
8. George
9. Ralph
10. Fred

a. Gracie
b. Lacey
c. Desi
d. Ernie
e. Alice
f. Laura
g. Lois
h. Ebert
i. Ethel
j. Jerry

Eve Arden

Quiz #16

OUR MISS BROOKS
(Answers on Page 130)

1. What was Miss Brooks' first name?

2. She taught at what high school?

3. What subject did she teach?

4. Name the principal of the high school.

5. What was his daughter's name?

6. Who was Miss Brooks' landlady?

7. Miss Brooks had a crush on which teacher?

8. What subject did he teach?

9. Who played that teacher?

10. Who was the school idiot?

Tony Randal – The Odd Couple

Bing Crosby and Jackie Mason

The singers on Your Hit Parade

Quiz #17

YOUR HIT PARADE
(Answers on Page 130)

1. How many years was *Your Hit Parade* on television?

2. Name the long-time sponsor.

3. Who sang the product every week?

4. Name the long-time orchestra leader.

5. Who was he married to?

6. What were the singers and dancers called?

7. Name the long-time announcer.

8. What caused the show to leave the air?

9. Name the singer on the show who was a classical violinist.

10. Who was the only singer on the show to have a top ten record?

The cast of Your Hit Parade

Quiz #18

TELEVISION SINGERS
(Answers on Page 131)

Match the hit song with the singer.

1. Eddie Fisher
2. Perry Como
3. Patti Page
4. Tennessee Ernie Ford
5. Andy Williams
6. Kate Smith
7. Frank Sinatra
8. Tony Orlando and Dawn
9. Bing Crosby
10. Rosemary Cooney

a. "New York, New York"
b. "God Bless America"
c. "Hey There"
d. "Oh, My Papa"
e. "Old Cape Cod"
f. "Moon River"
g. "Catch a Falling Star"
h. "White Christmas"
i. "Sixteen Tons"
j. "Sweet Gypsy Rose"

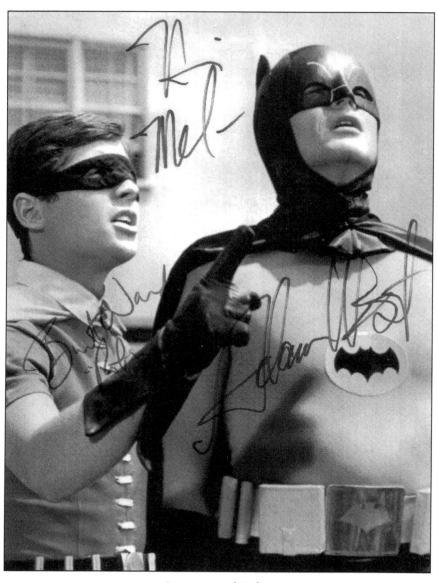

Batman and Robin

Quiz #19

BATMAN
(Answers on Page 131)

Match the character with the performer.

1. Mr. Freeze
2. The Catwoman
3. King Tut
4. The Riddler
5. Ma Parker
6. Louie the Lilac
7. The Joker
8. Lola Lasagne
9. Chandell
10. The Penguin

a. Frank Gorshin
b. George Sanders
c. Cesar Romero
d. Julie Newmar
e. Shelly Winters
f. Milton Berle
g. Burgess Meredith
h. Liberace
i. Victor Buono
j. Ethel Merman

First-day covers of television stars

Mitch Miller

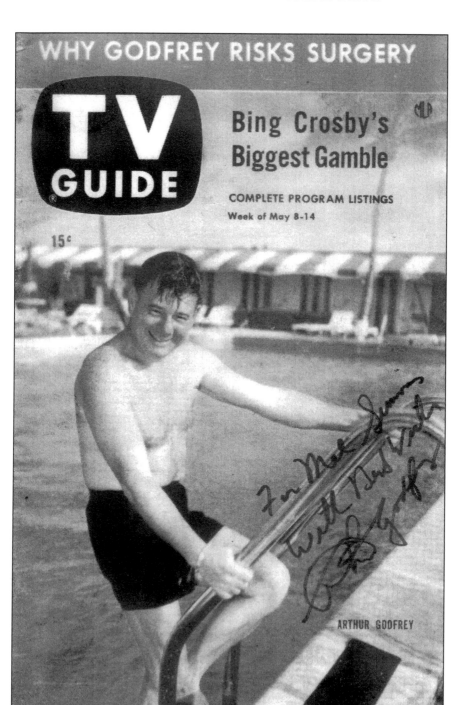

Arthur Godfrey

Quiz #20

ARTHUR GODFREY
(Answers on Page 131)

1. Name his evening show that was simulcast on both radio and television.

2. Name his morning show that was simulcast on both radio and television.

3. Who was his long-time announcer?

4. What was the name of his Wednesday night television show?

5. Name his long-time orchestra leader.

6. Who did Marion Marlowe sing duets with?

7. Julius La Rosa was in what branch of the service when Arthur discovered him?

8. Who was his Hawaiian singer?

9. Who was his Irish singer?

10. Arthur co-hosted what TV show with Allen Funt?

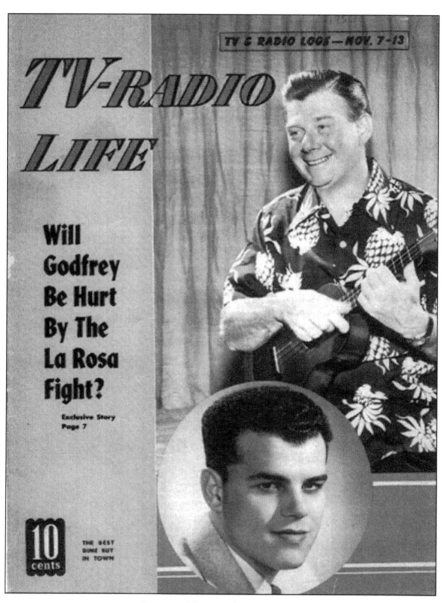

Arthur Godfrey and Julius La Rosa

Julius La Rosa

Liberace

Quiz #21

THEME SONGS
(Answers on Page 132)

Match the TV theme with the singer(s).

1. *The Loveboat*
2. *All in the Family*
3. *Chico and the Man*
4. *Welcome Back, Kotter*
5. *Baretta*
6. *Green Acres*
7. *"The Ballad of Jed Clampett"*
8. *Maude*
9. *The Dukes of Hazzard*
10. *Rawhide*

a. Sammy Davis, Jr.
b. Jack Jones
c. Eva Gabor and Eddie Albert
d. Frankie Laine
e. Donny Hathaway
f. Carroll O'Connor and Jean Stapleton
g. Jose Feliciano
h. Waylon Jennings
i. John Sebastion
j. Lester Flatt and Earl Scruggs

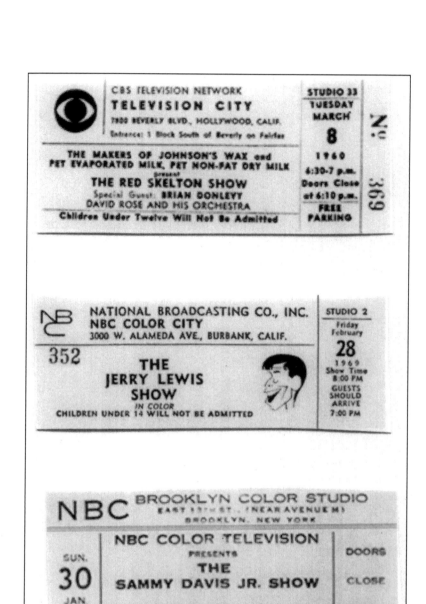

Tickets to television shows

Quiz #22

NAMES

(Answers on Page 132)

What are the last names of these personalities?

1. Irma

2. Lilly

3. Buffalo Bob

4. Luigi

5. Pepper

6. Maude

7. Clarabell

8. Lucy

9. Rhoda

10. Little Margie

Regis Philbin

Quiz #23

ORCHESTRA LEADERS
(Answers on Page 132)

Match the orchestra leader with the show's host.
1. Ray Bloch
2. David Rose
3. Doc Severinsen
4. Jose Melis
5. Bobby Rosengarden
6. Mort Lindsey
7. Johnny Mann
8. Archie Bleyer
9. Mitchell Ayres
10. Alan Roth

a. Perry Como
b. Merv Griffin
c. Johnny Carson
d. Jackie Gleason
e. Milton Berle
f. Jack Paar
g. Red Skelton
h. Joey Bishop
i. Dick Cavett
j. Arthur Godfrey

Penny arcade cards

Quiz #24

IDENTIFY THE NIGHT OF THE WEEK EACH SHOW WAS ON

(Answers on Page 133)

1. *The Andy Griffith Show*

2. *Your Show of Shows*

3. *The Garry Moore Show*

4. *The Life of Riley*

5. *Gunsmoke*

6. *The $64,000 Question*

7. *The Jackie Gleason Show*

8. *This is Your Life*

9. *60 Minutes*

10. *The Danny Thomas Show*

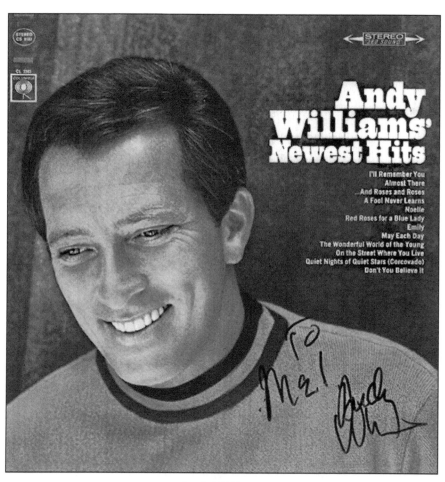

Andy Williams

Quiz #25

CATCH PHRASES
(Answers on Page 133)

Match the personality with his catch phrase.

1. "Gettum Up, Scout"
2. "The devil made me do it."
3. "So long until tomorrow."
4. "Good night and may God bless."
5. "Would you believe . . .?"
6. "Oooooh, what's gonna happen to him?"
7. "Who is buried in Grant's Tomb?"
8. "Ever notice . . ."
9. "Here's the dear boy himself."
10. "Strange things are happening."

a. Groucho Marx
b. Red Skelton
c. Don Adams
d. Tonto
e. Arthur Treacher
f. Lowell Thomas
g. Red Buttons
h. Ralph Edwards
i. Andy Rooney
j. Flip Wilson

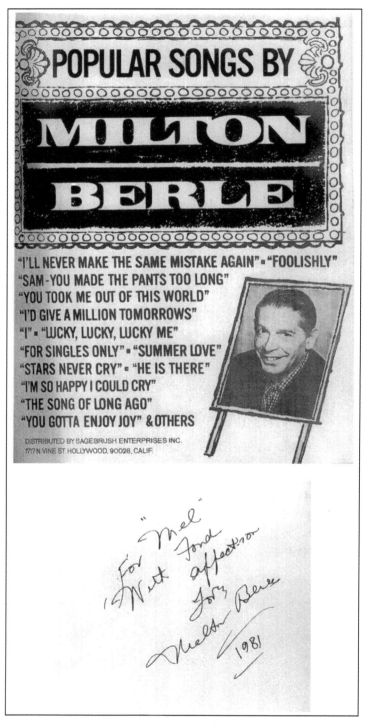

Milton Berle

Quiz #26

MILTON BERLE
(Answers on Page 133)

1. Milton entered show business at what age?

2. He got his start on radio on whose show?

3. Name his famous television show.

4. He signed a thirty-year contract with what network?

5. Who was his pitchman on the show who did the commercials?

6. What was the pitchman's most famous saying?

7. Name Milton's overweight second banana.

8. Milton's mother was a real stage mother. What was her first name?

9. What was Milton's nickname?

10. Name his theme song?

The Long Ranger and Tonto

Quiz #27

THE LONE RANGER
(Answers on Page 134)

1. Name the theme song of *The Lone Ranger*.

2. When Clayton Moore left the show for one year, who replaced him?

3. What was the Lone Ranger's real name?

4. Who created the show?

5. Name the Lone Ranger's nephew.

6. The nephew was the father of what character?

7. What kind of an Indian was Tonto?

8. Butch Cavendish was the leader of what gang?

9. As he rode away, what were the Lone Ranger's last words?

10. As he rode away, what were Tonto's last words?

The Lone Ranger

Quiz #28

GENERAL QUESTIONS
(Answers on Page 134)

1. Who played the flying nun?

2. Jack Jones sang the theme of what show?

3. Name the original host of *The Today Show*.

4. What was Mr. Peepers' first name?

5. The Osmond Brothers got their start on what television show?

6. Who played Lieutenant Columbo?

7. Name the most popular person on the center square of *The Hollywood Squares*.

8. What was the name of the cab company on *Taxi*?

9. Allen Funt created and hosted what TV show?

10. Who hosted *Death Valley Days*?

Mike Connors

Quiz #29

TELEVISION WESTERNS

(Answers on Page 134)

Match the actor with the TV Western.

1. James Arness
2. Chuck Connors
3. Gene Barry
4. James Garner
5. Guy Madison
6. Duncan Renaldo
7. Richard Boone
8. Clint Eastwood
9. Ward Bond
10. Jock Mahoney

a. *The Cisco Kid*
b. *Maverick*
c. *Rawhide*
d. *Gunsmoke*
e. *The Range Rider*
f. *Have Gun – Will Travel*
g. *Bat Masterson*
h. *The Rifleman*
i. *Wagon Train*
j. *Wild Bill Hickok*

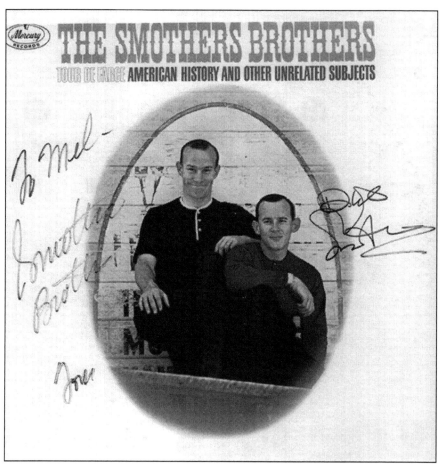

The Smothers Brothers

Quiz #30

WOMEN OF LAUGHTER
(Answers on Page 135)

Match the comedienne with her TV show.

1. Marlo Thomas
2. Betty White
3. Rhea Perlman
4. Isabel Sanford
5. Karen Valentine
6. Cindy Williams
7. Carolyn Jones
8. Nancy Walker
9. Dagmar
10. Eve Arden

a. *Rhoda*
b. *Cheers*
c. *That Girl*
d. *Lavern and Shirley*
e. *Our Miss Brooks*
f. *Broadway Open House*
g. *The Golden Girls*
h. *Room 222*
i. *The Jeffersons*
j. *The Addams Family*

Connie Stevens – Mel Simons – Piper Laurie

Quiz #31

PLACES OF ORIGIN
(Answers on Page 135)

Match the show with where the show took place.

1. *Dragnet*
2. *All in the Family*
3. *Cheers*
4. *Laverne and Shirley*
5. *M*A*S*H*
6. *I Dream of Jeannie*
7. *The Mary Tyler Moore Show*
8. *Surfside Six*
9. *Alice*
10. *Get Smart*

a. Boston, Massachusetts
b. Washington, D.C.
c. Miami Beach, Florida
d. Queens, New York
e. Phoenix, Arizona
f. Los Angeles, California
g. Milwaukee, Wisconsin
h. Korea
i. Minneapolis, Minnesota
j. Coco Beach, Florida

Chuck Connors – The Rifleman

Quiz #32

WHAT APPEARED WHERE?
(Answers on Page 135)

From the following fifteen shows:
Five appeared on radio and television
Five appeared on just television
Five appeared on radio, television and movies

1. *My Friend Irma*
2. *Law and Order*
3. *Gunsmoke*
4. *Cheers*
5. *Your Hit Parade*
6. *The Jeffersons*
7. *Superman*
8. *The Life of Riley*
9. *The Quiz Kids*
10. *Walter Winchell*
11. *Duffy's Tavern*
12. *Sing Along With Mitch*
13. *St. Elsewhere*
14. *Howdy Doody*
15. *Charlie Chan*

Carroll Spinney – Big Bird

Quiz #33

COMMERCIALS
(Answers on Page 136)

1. I want my _____.

2. Extra value is what you get when you use
   _____.

3. _____, what a chunk o' chocolate!

4. For taste and more it's _____.

5. _____ _____, they're magically
   delicious.

6. A day without _____ _____ is like
   a day without sunshine.

7. _____ is on your side.

8. I am stuck on _____ _____, and
   _____ _____ stuck on me.

9. Brusha-Brusha toothpaste, with _____
   tooth paste.

10. _____, the long lasting quicker picker upper.

Eddie Fisher

Quiz #34

EDDIE FISHER
(Answers on Page 136)

1. Where was Eddie born?

2. He was a production singer at what famous nightclub?

3. Who discovered Eddie and made him a star?

4. Name the resort in the Catskill Mountains where this took place?

5. Eddie's first appearance on television was on what show?

6. What record company did he record for?

7. What was his first number one record?

8. Name his biggest selling record.

9. Eddie hosted what television show?

10. Name his theme song on that show.

Ralph Bellamy – Man Against Crime

Quiz #35

GENERAL QUESTIONS
(Answers on Page 136)

1. The Anderson family appeared on what sitcom?

2. What was Dean Martin's theme song?

3. Name the puppet used by Wayland Flowers.

4. Who played the first Alice Kramden on *The Honeymooners*.

5. Miss Frances hosted what kids' show?

6. Name the first black performer to have his own network variety show.

7. Pinky Lee began his career in what branch of show business?

8. Who was Chet Huntley's partner?

9. *Sea Hunt* starred what personality?

10. Kukla, Fran and Ollie came from what city?

Duncan Renaldo – The Cisco Kid

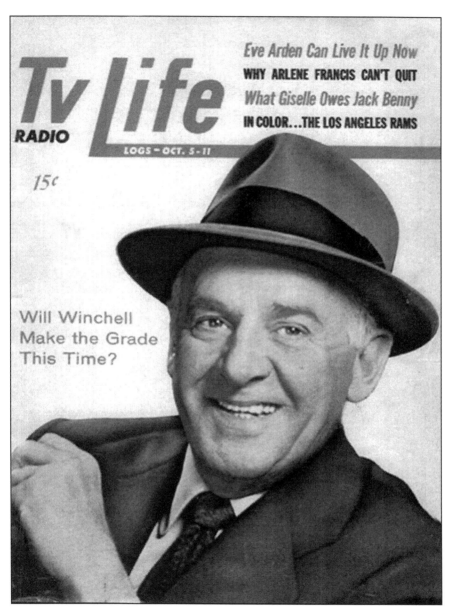

Walter Winchell

George Reeves and Noel Neill – Superman

Quiz #36

SUPERMAN
(Answers on Page 137)

1. Who created Superman?

2. Superman first appeared in what comic book?

3. What planet did Superman come from?

4. Clark Kent worked for what newspaper?

5. Name the editor of the newspaper.

6. What was his favorite expression?

7. Name the two ladies who played Lois Lane.

8. Who was the cub reporter?

9. Where did Superman live?

10. Name the long-time sponsor.

Art Linkletter

Spike Jones

Jack Benny and Rochester

Quiz #37

MATCH THE STARS WITH THEIR HIT RECORD

(Answers on Page 137)

1. Ricky Nelson
2. Merv Griffin
3. Shelley Fabares
4. Lorne Greene
5. Vicki Lawrence
6. Wink Martindale
7. Patty Duke
8. David Soul
9. Gale Storm
10. Tom Jones

a. "Deck of Cards"
b. "She's a Lady"
c. "Ringo"
d. "Johnny Angel"
e. "I Hear You Knocking"
f. "Travelin' Man"
g. "I've Got a Lovely Bunch of Coconuts"
h. "The Night the Lights Went Out in Georgia"
i. "Don't Just Stand There"
j. "Don't Give Up On Us"

Richard Webb – Captain Midnight

Quiz #38

ENDORSEMENTS
(Answers on Page 137)

Match the personality with the product they endorse.

1. Joe DiMaggio
2. Henry Fonda
3. Jane Withers
4. Lucy and Desi
5. Ed McMahon
6. Pat Boone
7. Andy Griffith
8. Arthur Godfrey
9. John Wayne
10. Homer and Jethro

a. Lipton Tea and Soup
b. Budweiser
c. Chevrolet
d. Mr. Coffee
e. Comet
f. Maxwell House Coffee
g. GAF
h. Philip Morris
i. American Cancer Society
j. Kellogg's Corn Flakes

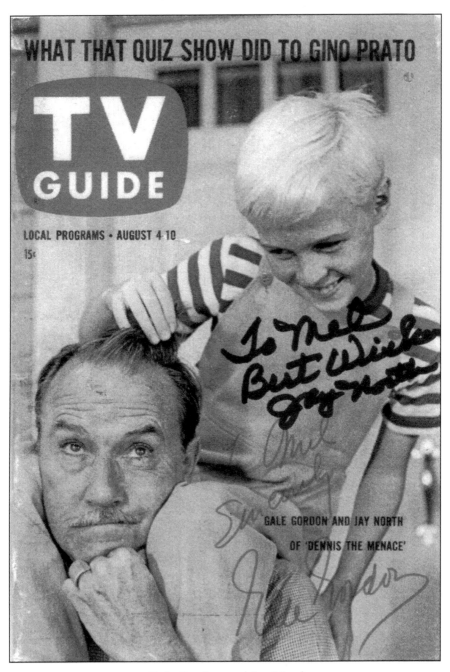

Gale Gordon and Jay North

Quiz #39

REAL NAMES
(Answers on Page 138)

Match the performer with his/her real name.

1. Red Buttons
2. Eve Arden
3. Larry King
4. Whoopie Goldberg
5. Dean Martin
6. Doris Day
7. Jack Benny
8. Shelly Winters
9. Monty Hall
10. Ginger Rogers

a. Eunice Quedens
b. Benjamin Kubelsky
c. Virginia McMath
d. Dino Crochetti
e. Karen Johnson
f. Laurence Zeiger
g. Shirley Shrift
h. Monte Halparin
i. Doris Van Kappelhoff
j. Aaron Chwatt

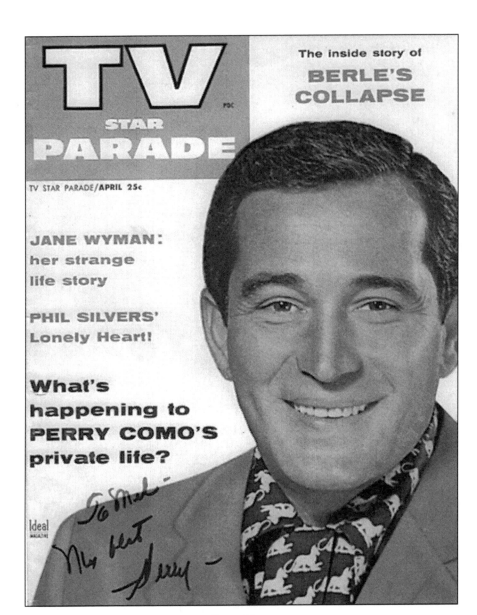

Perry Como

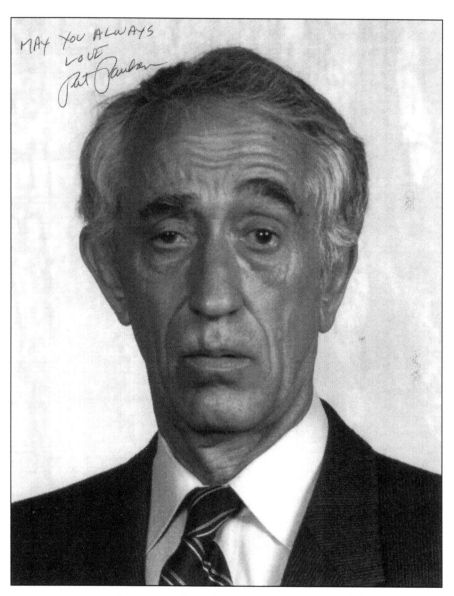

Pat Paulsen – The Smothers Brothers Comedy Hour

1950s magazines

Quiz #40

LADIES' NAMES
(Answers on Page 138)

Fill in the lady's first name.

1. *I Married _____.*

2. *The _____ Reed Show.*

3. *My Little _____.*

4. *_____ Hartman, _____ Hartman*

5. *A Date With _____*

6. *The _____ Sothern Show*

7. *My Friend _____*

8. *The _____ Burnett Show*

9. *My Sister _____*

10. *The Beautiful _____ Diller Show*

Sid Caesar and Imogene Coca

Quiz #41

CATCH PHRASES
(Answers on Page 138)

Match the personality with his catch phrase.

1. "Take my wife, please."
2. "Would you believe . . ."
3. "May I sing to you?"
4. "Hello, Dummy."
5. "Wait a minute."
6. "Here's Johnny."
7. "Uh one, and uh two"
8. "Same to you, fella."
9. "A really big shew"
10. "Hey, Lucy."

a. Jack Benny
b. Lawrence Welk
c. Ed Sullivan
d. Henny Youngman
e. Don Adams
f. Eddie Fisher
g. Desi Arnaz
h. Don Rickles
i. Bob Newhart
j. Ed McMahon

Imogene Coca

Quiz #42

MULTIPLE CHOICE
(Answers on Page 139)

1. What was the rank of Peter Falk on *Columbo*?
   a) Lieutenant   b) Captain   c) Private

2. Della Street was a character on which show?
   a) *The FBI*   b) *Ironside*   c) *Perry Mason*

3. Who hosted *Ding Dong School*?
   a) Miss Gans   b) Miss Frances   c) Miss Jenkins

4. What was the first name of *That Girl*?
   a) Ann   b) Marie   c) Ann Marie

5. The theme of *The Tonight Show* Starring Johnny Carson was written by whom?
   a) Neil Diamond   b) Paul Anka   c) Neil Diamond

6. *The Colgate Comedy Hour* featured whom?
   a) Eddie Cantor   b) Tony Martin   c) George Jessel

7. What early rock song was the theme for *Happy Days*?
   a) "Sh-Boom"   b) "Rock Around the Clock"
   c) "Blue Moon"

8. Name the Red Sox ballplayer who once appeared on *Cheers*.
   a) Pedro Morales   b) Fred Lynn   c) Wade Boggs

9. On *Saturday Night Live* Dana Carvey played whom?
   a) Church Lady   b) Joe Franklin   c) Cher

10. Name the first TV theme to reach #1 on the Billboard Chart.
    a) *S*W*A*T*   b) *Dragnet*   c) *I Love Lucy*

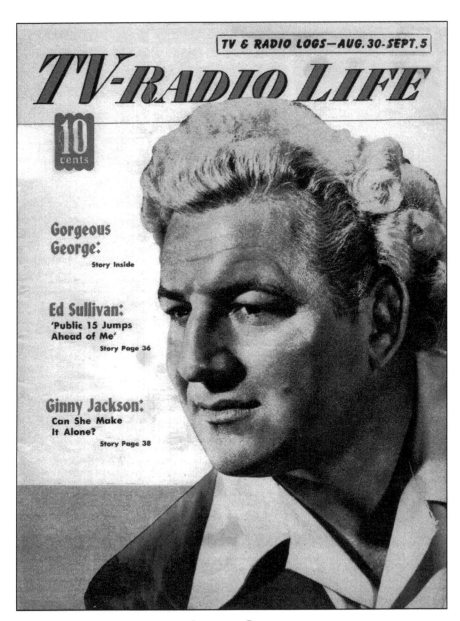

Gorgeous George

Quiz #43

NAMES
(Answers on Page 139)

What are the first names of these personalities?

1. Rockford

2. Mr. Peepers

3. Cannon

4. Topper

5. Riley

6. Mr. Rogers

7. Ironside

8. Mr. North

9. McCloud

10. Mr. Magoo

Paul Winchell and Jerry Mahoney

Linda Carter – Wonder Woman

The cast of Happy Days

Quiz #44

COMMERCIALS
(Answers on Page 139)

Match the product with the slogan.

1. The quicker picker upper
2. Bet you can't eat just one.
3. Finger lickin' good
4. Floats the dirt right down the drain
5. Good to the last drop
6. When you're number two, you have to try harder.
7. A little dab'll do ya.
8. 99 and 44-100 percent pure
9. Gets rid of dirt and grime and grease in just a minute
10. Breakfast of champions

a. Ajax
b. Bounty paper towels
c. Mr. Clean
d. Brylcreem
e. Wheaties
f. Avis Rent-a-Car
g. Kentucky Fried Chicken
h. Lay's Potato Chips
i. Maxwell House Coffee
j. Ivory Soap

Homes of television stars

Quiz #45

A LINE FROM A TV THEME
(Answers on Page 140)

Identify the TV show.

1. A horse is a horse, of course, of course.

2. Hey there, hi there, ho there, you're as welcome as can be.

3. A fiery horse with the speed of light

4. Boy, the way Glenn Miller played

5. Their house is a museum, where people come to see 'em.

6. Seems like old times.

7. The weather started getting rough, the tiny ship was tossed.

8. Let's give a rousing cheer.

9. Dream along with me.

10. I've got a gang, you've got a gang, everybody's got to have a gang.

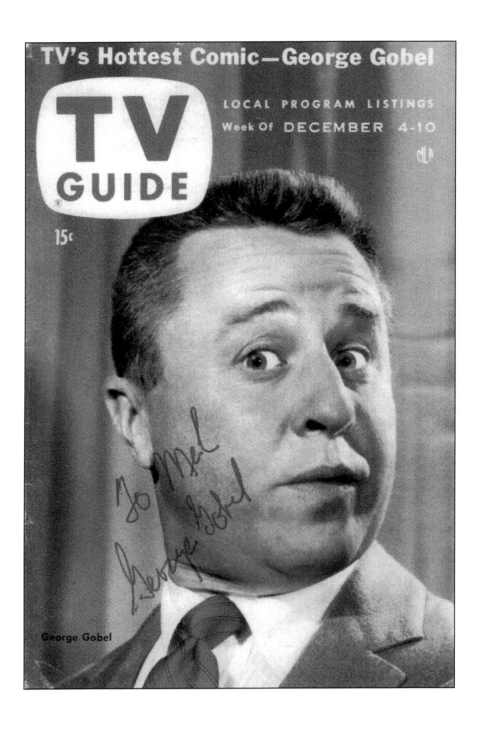

Tickets to television shows

Penny arcade cards

Quiz #46

NUMBERS
(Answers on Page 140)

Fill in the number.

1. *Car _____, Where Are You?*
2. *I Led _____ Lives*
3. *Surfside _____*
4. *_____ Men*
5. *Adam _____*
6. *_____th Precinct*
7. *Playhouse _____*
8. *The Roaring _____*
9. *_____ Sunset Strip*
10. *Route _____*

Tony Dow and Jerry Mathers – Leave It to Beaver

Quiz #47

TRUE OR FALSE
(Answers on Page 140)

1. Paul Anka wrote the theme for *The Tonight Show Starring Johnny Carson*.

2. Tonto, in real life, was a Mohawk Indian.

3. *TV Guide* was introduced in 1952.

4. James Stewart once had his own television show.

5. Dennis James once announced boxing.

6. Sonny Bono was once the mayor of Palm Beach.

7. A LUSH was the license plate for Foster Brooks.

8. The first host of *Good Morning, America* was David Hartman.

9. Jon Provost starred in *Rin Tin Tin*.

10. Ted Mack was the host of *The Original Amateur Hour* on both radio and television.

Peter Marshall – Hollywood Squares

Quiz #48

MULTIPLE CHOICE
(Answers on Page 141)

1. Who was Perry Como's announcer?
   a) Don Wilson   b) Frank Gallop   c) Harlow Wilson

2. Nat "King" Cole played which musical instrument?
   a) organ   b) accordion   c) piano

3. Charles Farrell was the co-star of what show?
   a) *My Little Margie*   b) *Gidget*   c) *I Married Joan*

4. Name the character played by Flip Wilson.
   a) Geraldine   b) Church Lady   c) Reverend Leroy

5. Who played Bob's wife on *The Bob Newhart Show*?
   a) Jayne Meadows   b) Suzanne Pleshette   c) Cher

6. Bob Emery was known as whom?
   a) The Lawman   b) Big Brother   c) The Count

7. TV Western show, Cheyenne, starred whom?
   a) John Wayne   b) Pat Brady   c) Clint Walker

8. Who had the "sweetest music this side of Heaven"?
   a) Sammy Kaye   b) Guy Lombardo
   c) Tommy Dorsey

9. Who was not a member of *The Monkeys*?
   a) Peter Tork   b) Peter Best   c) Mike Nesmith

10. Name the host of *What's My Line*?
    a) John Daly   b) Bill Cullen   c) Bud Collyer

I Love Lucy *gum cards*

Quiz #49

I LOVE LUCY
(Answers on Page 141)

1. Where was Desi born?

2. What was Lucy's maiden name?

3. Name Desi's nightclub.

4. Where was the nightclub located?

5. What was Desi's most famous song?

6. Name the Marx Brother who once appeared on the show.

7. Who played Ethel Mertz?

8. Lucy got drunk doing a commercial for what product?

9. What other sitcom did William Frawley star in?

10. The final season of the show, where did Lucy and Desi move to?

The cast of What's My Line?

Lindsay Wagner and Mel Simons

Erik Estrada and Mel Simons

The cast of Howdy Doody

Quiz #50

ROCK 'N' ROLL
(Answers on Page 141)

Match the rock group with the leader.

1. Bill Haley
2. Little Anthony
3. Martha
4. Buddy Holly
5. Tommy James
6. Dion
7. Paul Revere
8. Gerry
9. Diana Ross
10. Joey Dee

a. The Raiders
b. The Comets
c. The Supremes
d. The Pacemakers
e. The Starlighters
f. The Crickets
g. The Imperials
h. The Shondells
i. The Belmonts
j. The Vandellas

Homes of television stars

Answers

QUIZ #1 *(from page 5)*

1. a
2. b
3. b
4. c
5. a
6. c
7. b
8. b
9. c
10. a

QUIZ #2 *(from page 7)*

1. c
2. g
3. b
4. j
5. a
6. f
7. h
8. e
9. i
10. d

QUIZ #3 *(from page 9)*

1. the accordion
2. champagne music
3. the Aragon Ballroom
4. the Lennon Sisters
5. Dianne, Peggy, Kathy, and Janet
6. Uh-one and uh-two
7. Alice Lon
8. Dodge
9. George Cates
10. Bobby Burgess

QUIZ #4 *(from page 11)*

1. Richard
2. twenty years
3. "Holiday For Strings"
4. David Rose
5. Cauliflower McPugg
6. Willie Lump Lump
7. Guzzler's Gin
8. Gertrude and Heathcliff
9. clowns
10. "Good night, and may God bless."

QUIZ #5 *(from page 13)*

1. d
2. h
3. e
4. i
5. c
6. j
7. f
8. a
9. g
10. b

QUIZ #6 *(from page 17)*

1. f
2. c
3. h
4. g
5. b
6. a
7. e
8. j
9. d
10. i

QUIZ #7 *(from page 19)*

1. b
2. f
3. h
4. j
5. e
6. i
7. d
8. a
9. c
10. g

QUIZ #8 *(from page 21)*

1. Cecil
2. William Frawley
3. *Strike It Rich*
4. Rosalie and Sammy
5. "When the Moon Comes Over the Mountain"
6. *The Love Boat*
7. Charmin
8. *The Millionaire*
9. a peacock
10. *Mickey Mouse Club*

QUIZ #9 *(from page 22)*
1. Tuesday
2. Tuesday
3. Sunday
4. Thursday
5. Saturday
6. Wednesday
7. Sunday
8. Tuesday and Thursday
9. Saturday
10. Monday

QUIZ #10 *(from page 23)*
1. Burr Tillstrom
2. J. Fred Muggs
3. *Highway Patrol*
4. Soupy Sales
5. Ken Murray
6. He was a comedy writer.
7. *I Married Joan*
8. *Surfside Six*
9. Rod Serling
10. cigars

QUIZ #11 *(from page 25)*
1. Toledo, Ohio
2. Amos Jacobs
3. *The Jazz Singer*
4. *Make Room For Daddy*
5. Wife – Jean Hagen, daughter – Sherry Jackson
6. Wife – Marjorie Lord, son – Rusty Hammer, daughter – Angela Cartwright
7. Uncle Tonoose
8. The Copa Club
9. Charlie Halpern
10. St. Jude Children's Research Hospital

QUIZ #12 *(from page 29)*

1. False (The sponsor was Maxwell House.)
2. True
3. False (Truman was the first.)
4. False (He was born in Nebraska.)
5. True
6. False (He was the president of NBC.)
7. True
8. True
9. False (Eddie Fisher had the hit.)
10. True

QUIZ #13 *(from page 31)*

1. f
2. b
3. e
4. d
5. i
6. a
7. g
8. j
9. c
10. h

QUIZ #14 *(from page 33)*

1. *You'll Never Get Rich*
2. Nat Hiken
3. Ernie Bilco
4. Sergeant
5. Fort Baxter
6. Kansas
7. Doberman
8. gamble
9. Colonel John Hall
10. Joan Hall

QUIZ #15 *(from page 35)*

1. c
2. g
3. h
4. j
5. f
6. d
7. b
8. a
9. e
10. i

QUIZ #16 *(from page 37)*

1. Connie
2. Madison High School
3. English
4. Osgood Conklin
5. Harriet
6. Mrs. Davis
7. Mr. Boynton
8. Biology
9. Robert Rockwell
10. Stretch Snodgrass

QUIZ #17 *(from page 41)*

1. 8 years (1950 – 1957)
2. Lucky Strike
3. Dorothy Collins
4. Raymond Scott
5. Dorothy Collins
6. The Hit Paraders and The Hit Parade Dancers
7. Andre Baruch
8. the popularity of rock 'n' roll music
9. Gisele MacKenzie
10. Gisele MacKenzie ("Hard to Get")

QUIZ #18 *(from page 43)*

1. d
2. g
3. e
4. i
5. f
6. b
7. a
8. j
9. h
10. c

QUIZ #19 *(from page 45)*

1. b
2. d
3. i
4. a
5. e
6. f
7. c
8. j
9. h
10. g

QUIZ #20 *(from page 49)*

1. *Arthur Godfrey's Talent Scouts*
2. *Arthur Godfrey Time*
3. Tony Marvin
4. *Arthur Godfrey and His Friends*
5. Archie Bleyer
6. Frank Parker
7. the Navy
8. Haleloke
9. Carmel Quinn
10. *Candid Camera*

QUIZ #21   *(from page 53)*

1. b
2. f
3. g
4. i
5. a
6. c
7. j
8. e
9. h
10. d

QUIZ #22   *(from page 55)*

1. Peterson
2. Mrs. Munster
3. Smith
4. Basco
5. Anderson
6. Finley
7. Hornblow
8. Ricardo
9. Morgenstern
10. Albright

QUIZ #23   *(from page 57)*

1. d
2. g
3. c
4. f
5. i
6. b
7. h
8. j
9. a
10. e

QUIZ #24 *(from page 59)*

1. Monday
2. Saturday
3. Tuesday
4. Friday
5. Saturday
6. Tuesday
7. Saturday
8. Wednesday
9. Sunday
10. Monday

QUIZ #25 *(from page 61)*

1. d
2. j
3. f
4. b
5. c
6. h
7. a
8. i
9. e
10. g

QUIZ #26 *(from page 63)*

1. age five
2. Rudy Vallee
3. *The Texaco Star Theater*
4. NBC
5. Sid Stone
6. "You say you want more for your money? Tell ya what I'm gonna do!"
7. Fatso Marco
8. Sadie (She later changed it to Saundra.)
9. Uncle Miltie
10. "Near You"

QUIZ #27   *(from page 65)*

1. "William Tell Overture"
2. John Hart
3. John Reid
4. George W. Trendle and Fran Striker
5. Dan Reid
6. The Green Hornet
7. a Mohawk Indian
8. the Hole in the Wall Gang
9. "Hi-yo, Silver!"
10. "Get um' up, Scout."

QUIZ #28   *(from page 67)*

1. Sally Field
2. *The Love Boat*
3. Dave Garroway
4. Robinson
5. *The Andy Williams Show*
6. Peter Falk
7. Paul Lynde
8. The Sunshine Taxi Company
9. *Candid Camera*
10. Ronald Reagan

QUIZ #29   *(from page 69)*

1. d
2. h
3. g
4. b
5. j
6. a
7. f
8. c
9. i
10. e

QUIZ #30 *(from page 71)*

1. c
2. g
3. b
4. i
5. h
6. d
7. j
8. a
9. f
10. e

QUIZ #31 *(from page 73)*

1. f
2. d
3. a
4. g
5. h
6. j
7. i
8. c
9. e
10. b

QUIZ #32 *(from page 75)*

RADIO AND TELEVISION	TELEVISION
Your Hit Parade	*Cheers*
Walter Winchell	*The Jeffersons*
The Quiz Kids	*St. Elsewhere*
Gunsmoke	*Law and Order*
Howdy Doody	*Sing Along With Mitch*

RADIO, TELEVISION AND MOVIES

My Friend Irma	*The Life of Riley*
Charlie Chan	*Duffy's Tavern*
Superman	

QUIZ #33 *(from page 77)*

1. Maypo
2. Coronet
3. Chunky
4. On-Cor
5. Lucky Charms
6. Orange Juice
7. Nationwide
8. Band Aids
9. Ipana
10. Bounty

QUIZ #34 *(from page 79)*

1. Philadelphia
2. The Copacabana
3. Eddie Cantor
4. Grossingers
5. *The Colgate Comedy Hour*
6. R.C.A.
7. "Wish You Were Here"
8. "Oh, My Papa"
9. *Coke Time*
10. "May I Sing to You?"

QUIZ #35 *(from page 81)*

1. *Father Knows Best*
2. "Everybody Loves Somebody Sometime"
3. Madame
4. Pert Kelton
5. *Ding Dong School*
6. Nat "King" Cole
7. Burlesque
8. David Brinkley
9. Lloyd Bridges
10. Chicago

QUIZ #36 *(from page 85)*

1. Jerry Siegel and Joe Shuster
2. Action Comics
3. Krypton
4. The Daily Planet
5. Perry White
6. "Great Caesar's ghost!"
7. Phyllis Coates and Noel Neil
8. Jimmy Olsen
9. Metropolis
10. Kellogg's cereals

QUIZ #37 *(from page 89)*

1. f
2. g
3. d
4. c
5. h
6. a
7. i
8. j
9. e
10. b

QUIZ #38 *(from page 91)*

1. d
2. g
3. e
4. h
5. b
6. c
7. f
8. a
9. i
10. j

QUIZ #39 *(from page 93)*

1. j
2. a
3. f
4. e
5. d
6. i
7. b
8. g
9. h
10. c

QUIZ #40 *(from page 97)*

1. Joan
2. Donna
3. Margie
4. Mary, Mary
5. Judy
6. Ann
7. Irma
8. Carol
9. Eileen
10. Phyllis

QUIZ #41 *(from page 99)*

1. d
2. e
3. f
4. h
5. a
6. j
7. b
8. i
9. c
10. g

QUIZ #42 *(from page 101)*

1. a
2. c
3. b
4. c
5. b
6. a
7. b
8. c
9. a
10. a

QUIZ #43 *(from page 103)*

1. Jim
2. Robinson
3. Frank
4. Cosmo
5. Chester
6. Fred
7. Robert
8. Jerry
9. Sam
10. Quincy

QUIZ #44 *(from page 107)*

1. b
2. h
3. g
4. a
5. i
6. f
7. d
8. j
9. c
10. e

QUIZ #45 *(from page 109)*

1. *Mr. Ed*
2. *Mickey Mouse Club*
3. *The Lone Ranger*
4. *All in the Family*
5. *The Addams Family*
6. *Arthur Godfrey Time*
7. *Gilligan's Island*
8. *Howdy Doody*
9. *Perry Como*
10. *Smilin' Ed's Gang* (later *Andy's Gang*)

QUIZ #46 *(from page 113)*

1. 54
2. 3
3. 6
4. 2 ½
5. 12
6. 87
7. 90
8. 20s
9. 77
10. 66

QUIZ #47 *(from page 115)*

1. True
2. True
3. False (It was introduced in 1953)
4. True
5. False (He announced wrestling.)
6. False (He was the mayor of Palm Springs.)
7. True
8. True
9. False (He starred in *Lassie*.)
10. True

QUIZ #48 *(from page 117)*

1. b
2. c
3. a
4. a & c
5. b
6. b
7. c
8. b
9. b
10. a

QUIZ #49 *(from page 119)*

1. Cuba
2. McGillicuddy
3. The Tropicana
4. Manhattan
5. "Babalu"
6. Harpo
7. Vivian Vance
8. Vitameatavegamin vitamins
9. *My Three Sons*
10. Connecticut

QUIZ #50 *(from page 123)*

1. b
2. g
3. j
4. f
5. h
6. i
7. a
8. d
9. c
10. e

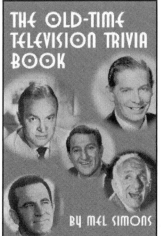

MEL

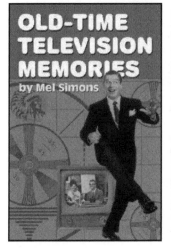

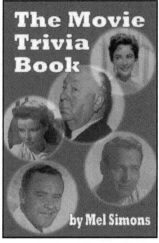

Available at
bearmanormedia.
com or at
MelSimons.net

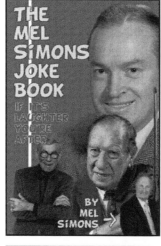

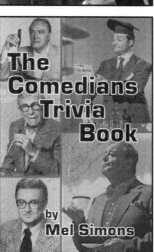

Made in the USA
Middletown, DE
04 June 2017